# Table of Contents

Introduction

**- Guidelines for Using the Journal**

**- Understanding the Reasons you Fast and Pray.**

**-Importance of Prayer and Fasting.**

Day 1: Initiating Connection

Day 2: Making Your Request Known

Day 3: Continuing with Petitions

Day 4: Discerning God's voice

Day 5: Resisting Temptations

Day 6: Intense Focus

Day 7: Reflective Meditation-Engaging with God's word

Day 8: Sustaining Spiritual Resilience

Day 9: Seeking a Deeper Connection with God

Day 10: Prayer and Confidence

Day 11: Gratitude Journaling

Day 12: Personal Praise and Worship

Day 13: Overcoming the Urge to Quit

*Day 14: Sharing Your Story*

*Day 15: Engaged Listening*

*Day 16: Renewed Purpose and Vision*

*Day 17: The fruits of the Spirit*

*Day 18: Giving in Order to Receive (Sacrifice)*

*Day 19: Prepared to Accept*

*Day 20: Ready to Receive*

*Day 21: Embracing Renewal*

## **Introduction**

*Welcome to your 21- day journey of prayer and fasting. This journal is designed to guide you through a transformative experience of drawing closer to God, renewing your spirit, and seeking his direction for your life.*

*In a world filled with noise and distractions, setting aside intentional time for prayer and fasting is a powerful way to align your heart with God's purposes and deepen your relationship with him. Throughout history, fasting has been a spiritual discipline practiced by people of faith to seek God's guidance, experience breakthroughs, and grow in intimacy with him.*

*As you start this journey, it is important to understand the purpose and significance of prayer and fasting. Fasting is not merely about abstaining from food; it's about feasting on God's presence. It's a time of consecration, surrender, and spiritual renewal. Through fasting, you deny yourself the comforts of the flesh to focus your attention on the things of the Spirit.*

*During these 21 days, you'll have the opportunity to engage in prayer, meditation, and reflection as you seek God's face corporately and individually. Each day, you'll find devotional readings, scripture verses, prayer prompts, and journaling space to guide you on this journey of spiritual growth and discovery.*

*I believe that as you commit yourself to this time of seeking God wholeheartedly, you will experience his presence in a profound way. Whether you're embarking on your first fast or you're a seasoned veteran, may this journal be a catalyst for transformation, breakthrough, and revival in your life.*

*Let's press in, pray fervently, and expectantly wait on the Lord together. May these 21 days be a season of encounter, revelation, and empowerment as we draw near to the heart of God.*

*Blessings on your journey,*

*Yours truly -Romario Smith*

## **Guidelines**

*Following these guidelines will help you make the most of your prayer and fasting experience and deepen your relationship with God.*

### 1. **Set Intentions**:

*Clarify your goals and purpose for the journey.*

### 2. **Stay Consistent:**

*Dedicate regular time each day for prayer and reflection.*

### 3. **Follow the Structure**:

*Engage with the daily readings, prompts, and reflections provided.*

### 4. **Be Open and Receptive**:

*Allow God to speak to you and guide your journey.*

### 5. **Be Honest and Vulnerable**:

*Share your thoughts and emotions authentically.*

## 6. *Journal Regularly:*

*Record your experiences and insights in your journal.*

## 7. *Seek Support:*

*Share your journey with trusted friends or mentors for encouragement.*

## 8. *Extend Grace*:

*Be patient with yourself and trust in God's faithfulness.*

## _Understanding the reasons you fast._

*Understanding the Reasons you fast and pray, emphasizes the purpose behind engaging in fasting and prayer. It suggests that before embarking on a journey of fasting and prayer, it's important to understand why you do so. This understanding helps guide your approach and mindset throughout the fasting and prayer period.*

- **"Proverb 4:7 -Wisdom is the principal thing; therefore, get wisdom: and with all thy getting, get understanding."**

*The accompanying Bible verse from Proverbs 4:7 highlights the importance of seeking wisdom and understanding. It suggests that gaining understanding is essential, even if it requires significant effort and sacrifice. In the context of fasting and prayer, this verse encourages seekers to approach their spiritual practices with a desire to gain insight and understanding into their faith, their relationship with God, and the reasons behind their fasting and prayer efforts.*

*Overall, the combination of the title and the Bible verse sets the tone for the journal by emphasizing the significance of understanding the reasons for fasting and prayer and seeking wisdom in this spiritual endeavor.*

*A comprehensive comprehension of the rationale behind fasting and prayer is fundamental for efficaciously engaging in these spiritual disciplines. Here are further insights to elucidate this point.*

**1. Clarity of Purpose:** *Understanding why you fast and pray provides clarity of purpose and motivation in your spiritual journey.*

**2. Alignment with Intentions:** *It ensures that your intentions for fasting, and prayer align with God's desires, strengthening your relationship with Him.*

**3. Deeper Spiritual Connection:** *Fasting and prayer offer opportunities to deepen your connection with God, fostering sincerity and expectation in your approach.*

**4.Personal Transformation:** *Engaging in fasting and prayer with understanding opens you to personal growth and transformation in line with God's will.*

**5. Enhanced Discipline:** *Understanding the significance of fasting and prayer helps you to maintain discipline and perseverance in your spiritual practices*

**6. *Cultivation of Wisdom:*** *Through fasting and prayer, you gain insights into yourself, your relationship with God, and His plans for your lives, cultivating wisdom and understanding.*

## What is your expectation for these 21 days of fasting and prayer?

*Journal space*

..............................................................................................

..............................................................................................

..............................................................................................

..............................................................................................

..............................................................................................

..............................................................................................

..............................................................................................

..............................................................................................

..............................................................................................

..............................................................................................

..............................................................................................

..............................................................................................

..............................................................................................

..............................................................................................

..............................................................................................

..............................................................................................

**Write 12 things you would like to accomplish throughout these 21 days of fasting and prayer.**

*Journal space*

## Day 1: Initiating Connection

**Scripture Focus:**

*"Jeremiah 29:13 - "You will seek me and find me when you seek me with all your heart."*

**Study and Application:**

*This verse emphasizes on the importance of sincere and wholehearted seeking of God. Here's and explanation:*

- **Seeking God**- *The act of seeking God implies a deliberate effort to know Him better, to understand His will, and to cultivate a deeper relationship with Him. It involves seeking His presence, wisdom and guidance in every aspect of life.*

- **Finding God**- *The promise in the verse is that when you seek God with all your heart, you will find Him. This finding goes beyond just discovering facts about God; it encompasses experiencing His presence, receiving His love and grace, and understanding His purpose for your life.*

- **Wholeheartedness**- *Seeking God with all your heart means doing so sincerely, earnestly and* with genuine passion. It requires putting aside distractions, doubts and half-hearted efforts, and instead, approaching God with openness, faith and devotion.

Take time to study the context of Jeremaih 29:13 within the larger narrative of God's promise to His people, then immerse yourself in this foundational verse emphasizing on the profound connection between wholehearted seeking and divine encounters.

Reflect on the significance of seeking God with all your heart. Consider what it means to approach God with sincerity, devotion, and undivided attention. Explore the implications of this verse for your own spiritual journey and relationship with God.

- **As you meditate on Jeremiah 29:13, ask yourself these (4) probing questions:**


- *- What does it mean to seek God with all my heart?*
- *- How does wholehearted seeking differ from casual or half-hearted efforts?*

- *- In what ways do distractions or competing priorities hinder my ability to seek God wholeheartedly?*
- *- What motivates me to seek God, and how can I cultivate a deeper longing for His presence?*

*Take time to journal your reflections, insights, and questions. Allow the Holy Spirit to guide your thoughts and reveal areas of your life where you may need to deepen your pursuit of God.*

- **Its Prayer and Reflection time:**

**1.** *Begin your prayer time by expressing gratitude to God for His promise to be found by those who seek Him wholeheartedly.*

**2.** *Confess any areas of your life where you have not pursued God with sincerity or devotion.*

**3.** *Ask God to ignite a passionate desire within you to seek Him with all your heart.*

**4.** *Pray for insight and revelation as you embark on this journey of wholehearted seeking.*

- ***Reflection points:***

**1. Understanding the Verse:** *Reflect on what it means to seek God with all your heart and why this is important in your relationship with Him.*

**2. Personal Reflection:** *Think about times when you've felt closest to God and how wholehearted seeking played a role. Consider any obstacles that have hindered your pursuit of God in the past.*

**3. Identifying Barriers**: *Identify any distractions or challenges that make it difficult for you to seek God with all your heart. Think about practical steps you can take to overcome these barriers.*

**4. Planning:** *Develop a simple plan for incorporating wholehearted seeking into your daily life. This could include setting aside specific time for prayer and Bible reading or finding ways to eliminate distractions during your quiet time.*

**Journaling and Reflection:**

*Wrap up your study session by jotting down your reflections, thoughts, and plans. Contemplate how God has communicated with you through His word and brainstorm actionable steps you can implement to incorporate these teachings into your daily life. Leverage your journal as a means of continuous introspection and personal development as you strive to seek God wholeheartedly.*

*Journal space*

## Day 2: Making Your Request Known

### Scripture Focus:

Philippians 4:6 - "Do not be anxious about anything, but in every situation, by prayer and petition, with thanksgiving, present your requests to God."

### Study and Application:

Delve into Philippians 4:6 with anticipation, recognizing it as a profound invitation to engage with God in the realm of prayer. This verse teaches us not to worry about anything but to pray about everything. We should talk to God, ask Him for what we need, and thank Him for what He has done. This verse serves to remind you to trust God with your worries and to be grateful in every situation.

### Unlock the depths of this scripture by pondering:

- **Avoid Anxiety**- The verse advises against letting worries and anxieties consume you. Instead of being overwhelmed by concerns, you should turn to prayer as a source of comfort and strength.

- **Pray About Everything**- Rather than keeping your worries to yourself, the verse encourages *you to bring everything to God in prayer. This includes your needs, concerns, hopes and desires. Prayer is seen as a powerful tool for communication and connection with God.*

- ***Gratitude and Trust**- Alongside prayer, the verse highlights the importance of gratitude and trust. you are encouraged to approach God with thanksgiving, acknowledging His goodness and faithfulness. By trusting God with your worries and expressing gratitude, you can find peace and assurance in His care.*

*As you immerse yourself in these reflections, allow the Holy Spirit to unveil new dimensions of truth and revelation.*

**Reflection Questions**: *Take a few minutes to think about your answer.*

- *Do I really trust God? () yes () no () I'm not sure.*

**Its Prayer and Reflection time:**

*1. Commence your prayer time with a posture of gratitude, acknowledging God's unwavering faithfulness and provision.*

*2. Candidly lay bare any areas of anxiety or apprehension that linger in your heart.*

*3. With boldness and expectancy, articulate your specific requests to God, surrendering them into His capable hands.*

*4. Let thanksgiving permeate your prayers, as you anticipate God's faithful response and provision in every circumstance.*

**Reflection points:**

**1.** *Dive into the transformative implications of relinquishing anxiety in every situation, contemplating how this aligns with God's character and promises.*

**2.** *Reflect on the nuanced differences between prayer and petition, discerning how each facet contributes to a holistic engagement with God.*

**3.** *Unpack the profound significance of thanksgiving in prayer, exploring how cultivating a heart of gratitude can shift your perspective and invite divine intervention.*

**4.** *Craft a personalized strategy for embodying Philippians 4:6 in your daily life, infusing your prayers with a spirit of trust, expectancy, and thanksgiving.*

***Journaling and Reflection:***

*Conclude your study session by chronicling your newfound insights and revelations in your journal. Document your prayers, petitions, and expressions of gratitude, anchoring them in the truth of God's Word. May your journal serve as a testimony to God's faithfulness and provision as you journey deeper into His presence.*

## Journal space

## **_Day 3: Continuing with Petitions_**

### **Scripture Focus:**

1 Thessalonians 5:16-18 - "Rejoice always, pray continually, give thanks in all circumstances; for this is God's will for you in Christ Jesus."

### **Study and Application:**

1 Thessalonians 5:16-18 is a passage that emphasizes the importance of joy, constant prayer, and gratitude in the Christian faith. Here's a breakdown of each verse:

- **Rejoice evermore:** This verse encourages believers to maintain a continuous state of joy or happiness. It implies that regardless of circumstances, believers should find reasons to be joyful, often linked to their faith and relationship with God.

- **Pray without ceasing:** This verse highlights the significance of constant communication with God through prayer. It doesn't necessarily mean praying every single moment but rather maintaining a lifestyle characterized by frequent and ongoing prayer, where one is always connected to God in conversation and communion.

- **In everything give thanks**: This verse underscores the importance of gratitude. It teaches believers to be thankful not just for the good things in life but also in all situations, including challenges and hardships. The perspective here is that gratitude should be a fundamental attitude of the heart, acknowledging God's sovereignty and goodness regardless of circumstances.

- The passage reflects a deep spiritual mindset that is centered on joy, prayerfulness, and gratitude, aligning one's life with the will of God as revealed through Jesus Christ.

**Reflection Questions:**

*1.* How can I cultivate a spirit of rejoicing always, even in the midst of difficult circumstances?

*2.* What practical steps can I take to incorporate continual prayer into my daily routine?

*3.* In what areas of my life do I struggle to give thanks in all circumstances, and how can I shift my perspective?

*4.* How can I align my life more closely with God's will for me, as revealed in 1 Thessalonians 5:16-18?

**Its Prayer and Reflection Time:**

*1.* Start your prayer time by rejoicing in the unchanging character and faithfulness of God, finding peace and strength in His everlasting presence.

*2.* Embrace prayer as a sacred practice that transcends mere words, permeating every facet of your existence, as you seek to deepen your communion with the God.

*3.* Offer prayers of heartfelt gratitude, recognizing God's hand at work in every circumstance, whether joyous or challenging, as you surrender your will to His divine plan.

**4.** Seek God's guidance and empowerment to live out His will for your life, rejoicing always, praying continually, and giving thanks in all circumstances.

### Analytical Inquiry:

- Reflect on the revolutionary call to rejoice always, discerning its profound implications for our spiritual posture and resilience in the face of adversity.

- Contemplate the transformative power of continual prayer, exploring practical strategies to cultivate an ongoing dialogue with God throughout your day.

- Meditate on the radical practice of giving thanks in all circumstances, recognizing its capacity to shift our focus from trials to triumphs, from despair to hope.

- *Craft a personalized roadmap for integrating these revelations into your daily rhythm, aligning your life with God's divine will for a joy-filled, prayerful, and gratitude-infused existence.*

### Journaling and Reflection:

*Conclude your study session by chronicling the revelations and insights gleaned from your exploration of 1 Thessalonians 5:16-18. Pour out your heart in prayer, recording your deepest aspirations, petitions, and expressions of gratitude. May your journal serve as a sacred repository of divine encounters and transformative revelations, guiding you ever closer to God's heart.*

*Journal space*

## Day 4: Discerning God's Voice

**Scripture Focus:**

John 10:27 - "My sheep listen to my voice; I know them, and they follow me."

**Study and Application:**

Commence your journey by deepening your ability to discern God's voice, as emphasized in John 10:27. This verse presents a powerful image of intimacy and connection between the Shepherd and His sheep, highlighting the reciprocal relationship of listening and following. As you reflect on this scripture, consider:

- *The invitation to cultivate a posture of attentiveness and receptivity to God's voice, recognizing it as a vital aspect of your relationship with Him.*

- The assurance that God knows His children intimately, and they, in turn, recognize and respond to His voice.

- The transformative impact of following God obediently, trusting His guidance and direction in every aspect of your life.

- Reflect on how these insights resonate with your own journey of faith and how you can deepen your ability to discern God's voice in your daily walk.

**Reflection Questions:**

**1.** How have I experienced God's voice speaking to me in the past, and what patterns do I notice in how He communicates with me?

**2.** What obstacles or distractions hinder my ability to hear God's voice clearly, and how can I overcome them?

**3.** In what areas of my life do I struggle to follow God's leading, and what steps can I take to align my will with His?

***4.*** *How can I cultivate a deeper intimacy with God, that I may recognize His voice more readily and follow Him more faithfully?*

***Its Prayer and Reflection Time:***

**1.** Begin your prayer time by inviting the Holy Spirit to open your ears and heart to hear God's voice more clearly.

**2.** Reflect on moments when you have sensed God speaking to you, whether through Scripture, prayer, circumstances, or the stillness of your heart.

**3.** Surrender any areas of resistance or doubt, asking God to strengthen your faith and trust in His voice.

**4.** Pray for a deeper intimacy with God, that you may know Him more fully and follow Him more closely in obedience.

***Analytical Inquiry:***

- Reflect on the significance of being able to hear God's voice and understanding its implications for your relationship with Him and your journey of faith.

- *Contemplate the various ways in which God speaks to His children, identifying which channels resonate most deeply with your soul.*

- *Meditate on the importance of obedience in following God's voice, considering how it reflects your love and trust in Him.*

- *Develop practical strategies for cultivating a deeper sensitivity to God's voice and discerning His guidance amidst the noise and distractions of life.*

### Journaling and Reflection:

*End your study session by journaling your reflections on John 10:27 and the insights gained from your prayers and analytical inquiry. Consider practical steps you can take to deepen your ability to discern God's voice and follow His leading with confidence and trust. Use your journal as a sacred space for ongoing dialogue with God and reflection on His faithful provision and guidance in your life.*

*Journal space*

## Day 5: Resisting Temptations

**Scripture Focus:**

1 Corinthians 10:13 - "No temptation has overtaken you except what is common to mankind. And God is faithful; he will not let you be tempted beyond what you can bear. But when you are tempted, he will also provide a way out so that you can endure it."

**Breakdown of Scripture:**

- No temptation is unique to you; others have faced similar struggles.

  - Every temptation you have encountered has likely been experienced by others at some point in time. This shared aspect of human experience reminds you that you are not alone in your struggles. Whether it's resisting a craving, overcoming a difficult decision or battling with a personal weakness, someone, somewhere has faced, or maybe still facing similar or same.

- God is faithful; He won't allow you to be tempted beyond what you can handle.

- *God is trustworthy and will not allow you to face temptations that exceed your abilities. Essentially, it reassures you, that you can rely on God's strength and support to overcome and bear in mind, that God knows more about you than you know about yourself.*

- He will provide a way out so you can endure it without giving in to temptation.

- *God will always offer a solution or provide an opportunity to help you overcome temptation or adversity. This means that you can welcome His assistance and trust His guidance. Knowing that he will always make a path or a means of navigating you through your time of difficulty.*

**Testimonial 1:**

Joseph's Temptation (Genesis 39:6-12)

*Joseph, while serving in Potiphar's household, faced the seduction of Potiphar's wife. Despite her advances, Joseph remained faithful to God, refusing to sin against Him.*

**Testimonial 2:**

Jesus' Temptation in the Wilderness (Matthew 4:1-11)

During His time in the wilderness, Jesus faced Satan's temptations, including offers of power and glory. Yet, Jesus resisted each temptation, relying on God's Word and His commitment to obedience.

**Reflection Question:**

- Have you ever encountered a temptation that seemed overwhelming? How did you respond?

**Scenario:**

Imagine you have applied for a visa to travel overseas for an important conference that could significantly advance your career. However, as the waiting period extends, doubts and anxieties begin to cloud your mind. You receive an unexpected opportunity to expedite the process by using connections to bypass certain procedures, but doing so would compromise your integrity and go against your Christian values.

- *What would you do in this situation and why would you do it?*

*Record your answer in the journal space provided.*

**Additional Reflection:**

Reflect on how God's faithfulness and the examples of Joseph and Jesus inspire you to resist temptation. Consider the strategies they employed, such as reliance on God's Word and obedience, and how you can apply them to your own life.

**Prayer Points:**

Take time to pray, asking for:

1. The wisdom to make wise decisions.
2. The strength to overcome temptation.
3. Faith to stand in times of difficulties.
4. Courage to fight back and to challenge the challenges
5. Integrity to stay faithful.

## Journal space

## Day 6: Intense Focus

### Scripture Focus:

Colossians 3:2 - "Set your minds on things above, not on earthly things."

In a world surrounded by distraction on every angle, focusing on God and Heavenly things can be one of the hardest task for any believer, especially today. Having intense focus requires discipline, sacrifice and hard work. Set aside anything and everything that comes in the form of distraction. Even if this means isolating yourself and push to master the art of being focused. You must understand that it is at this point that the devil will try his outmost best to get you to lose focus; and this is often at your breakthrough point.

### Study and Application:

Reflect on the significance of redirecting your thoughts and focus on heavenly realities, as instructed in Colossians 3:2. Consider how prioritizing eternal truths over temporary concerns can lead to a deeper sense of purpose and alignment with God's will in your daily life. Explore practical ways to cultivate a mindset that is centered on heavenly matters, such as regular *scripture meditation, prayer, and intentional focus on God's kingdom principles.*

**Scriptures Supporting Focus on Heavenly Things:**

**1.** *Matthew 6:19-21 - "Do not store up for yourselves treasures on earth, where moths and vermin destroy, and where thieves break in and steal. But store up for yourselves treasures in heaven, where moths and vermin do not destroy, and where thieves do not break in and steal. For where your treasure is, there your heart will be also."*

**2.** *Philippians 4:8 - "Finally, brothers and sisters, whatever is true, whatever is noble, whatever is right, whatever is pure, whatever is lovely, whatever is admirable—if anything is excellent or praiseworthy—think about such things."*

**3.** *Romans 12:2 - "Do not conform to the pattern of this world but be transformed by the renewing of your mind. Then you will be able to test and approve what God's will is—his good, pleasing and perfect will."*

### Its Prayer and Reflection Time:

Begin your prayer time by surrendering your thoughts and desires to God, inviting Him to help you set your mind on things above. Confess any areas where earthly distractions have taken precedence in your life and ask for His guidance in aligning your thoughts with His will. Pray for clarity of mind, spiritual discernment, and a deepening desire to seek after the things that are pleasing to God. This should be your priority prayer points for the rest of the day.

- Here are some games to keep you active and help keep you focused on the task at hand.

### Game: Trash Bin Distraction Toss

Grab a piece of paper and a pen. Write down any distractions, worries, or earthly concerns that are occupying your mind. Take a moment to acknowledge them, but then crumple up the paper and toss it into a nearby trash bin. As you do this, visualize releasing these distractions into God's hands, trusting Him to handle them. Feel a sense of relief as you let go of these burdens and redirect your focus to heavenly realities.

### Game: Bible Verse Focus

**1.** Choose a short Bible verse.

**2.** Read the verse aloud or silently to familiarize yourself with it.

**3**. Close your eyes and repeat the verse in your mind.

**4**. Open your eyes and try to write down the verse from memory.

**5**. Check the actual verse to see how well you remember it.

**6.** Reflect on your ability to focus and recall the verse.

**7**. Repeat with other verses to practice.

### Journaling and Reflection:

Conclude your study session by journaling your reflections on Colossians 3:2, the insights gained from your prayers, exploration, and your experiences with the Trash Bin Distraction Toss game. Consider how this simple activity helped you to release earthly concerns and refocus your mind on God's presence and eternal truths. Commit to *practicing this exercise regularly to maintain a mindset that is centered on things above and to experience greater peace and clarity in your daily life.*

*Journal space*

## Day 7: Reflective Meditation - Engaging with God's Word

### Scripture Focus:

Psalm 119:105 - "Your word is a lamp for my feet, a light on my path."

Today you spend quality time reflecting on the importance of God's word and how it has played a significant part in your walk of faith. Engage yourself today by answering these self-reflector questions. Take your time to answer each question as answering these questions will help to identify some of the issues you face while meditating.

### Multiple Choice Reflection:

Answering these questions will help to identify some of the issues while meditating.

1. How does meditating on God's Word impact your spiritual life?

   - a) Deepens relationship with God

- b) Provides guidance and direction

- c) Strengthens faith and trust

- d) All of the above

2. Which method is most helpful for meditating on Scripture?

   - a) Reading slowly and reflectively

   - b) Memorizing verses

   - c) Journaling insights

   - d) All of the above

3. What obstacles do you encounter when meditating on God's Word?

   - a) Distractions

   - b) Busy schedules

   - c) Feeling sleepy or falling asleep

   - d) All of the above

4. How do you respond to distractions during meditation?

- a) Refocus on Scriptures

- b) Become frustrated

- c) Acknowledge and refocus

- d) All of the above

5. Which benefits have you experienced from meditating on Scripture?

   - a) Peace and contentment

   - b) Understanding God's character

   - c) Insight into personal struggles

   - d) All of the above

6. How do you prioritize meditation on God's Word?

   - a) Schedule specific times

   - b) Integrate into daily activities

   - c) Set reminders

   - d) All of the above

7. What strategies do you use to maintain focus during meditation?

- a) Prayer

- b) Deep breathing

- c) Reading the Word

- d) All of the above

8. How does meditating on Scripture impact decision-making?

- a) Provides clarity

- b) Discerns God's will

- c) Guides moral choices

- d) All of the above

9. What role does Scripture memory play in meditation?

- a) Recalls key verses

- b) Deepens understanding

- c) Provides comfort

- d) All of the above

10. How do you respond to new insights during meditation?

   - a) By thanking God

   - b) Journal insights

   - c) Share with others

   - d) All of the above

11. In what ways does Scripture meditation affect your prayer life?

   - a) Deepens intimacy with God

   - b) Provides inspiration for prayers

   - c) Aligns prayers with God's will

   - d) All of the above

12. How do you incorporate Scripture meditation into daily activities?

   - a) Listening to audio Bible

   - b) Reflecting during walks

   - c) Integrating into chores

- d) All of the above

13. What benefits do you see from meditating on Scripture during challenging times?

    - a) Comfort and encouragement

    - b) Perspective and hope

    - c) Strength and resilience

    - d) All of the above

14. How does sharing insights from Scripture meditation impact your relationships?

    - a) Deepens connections

    - b) Provides encouragement

    - c) Sparks meaningful conversations

    - d) All of the above

15. What motivates you to continue meditating on Scripture?

- a) Growth in faith

   - b) Desire for wisdom

   - c) Hunger for God's presence

   - d) All of the above


16. How do you seek accountability and support in your Scripture meditation practice?

   - a) Joining a Bible study group

   - b) Partnering with a prayer buddy

   - c) Seeking guidance from a mentor

   - d) All of the above


17. How do you adjust your Scripture meditation practice during busy seasons?

   - a) Shorter, focused sessions

   - b) Integrating into daily routines

   - c) Prioritizing quiet moments

   - d) All of the above


18. What insights have you gained from Scripture meditation about your identity in Christ?

- a) Beloved child of God

- b) Chosen and redeemed

- c) Called to serve and love

- d) All of the above

19. How do you engage with different genres of Scripture during meditation?

- a) Reflecting on Psalms for worship

- b) Studying epistles for doctrine

- c) Contemplating narratives for lessons

- d) All of the above

20. How do you envision Scripture meditation shaping your future spiritual journey?

- a) Deeper intimacy with God

- b) Greater understanding of His Word

- c) Increased faith and reliance

- d) All of the above

The purpose of this questionnaire is to help you to identify possible areas in your life that you may need to tighten up. As you reflect on your answers, as yourself:

- What have I figured out and/or learn about me while answering these questions?
- Am I satisfied with my results?
- How can I help me to grow more?

Conclude this study and exploration by using the journal space provided to document any insights gained from today's experience. Ensure you are allowing yourself to be vulnerable and be as honest as possible, to be able to identify any areas of weakness in your walk of faith and work to improve yourself.

**Prayer Points:**

- Ask God to reveal any and every weak area in your life.

- Pray for strength and wisdom to make wise decisions.

- Pray that you will continue to be persistent and consistent in faith.

- Pray for a deeper connection with the Spirit of God so that He may order your steps in His Word.

*Journal space*

## Day 8: Sustaining Spiritual Resilience

### Scripture focus:

Isaiah 40:31 "but those who hope in the Lord shall renew their strength. They will soar on wings of eagle; they will run and not grow weary; they will walk and not be faint."

### Summary:

As you journey through Day 8 of your fasting and prayer regimen, the theme of sustaining spiritual resilience takes center stage. This pivotal moment in your spiritual quest calls for a deeper exploration of your inner strength and unwavering commitment to your faith journey.

At the break of dawn, you're awakened with renewed determination, setting the tone for the day ahead by reaffirming your dedication to spiritual growth and connection with God. With each breath, you infuse your intentions with clarity and purpose, anchoring yourself in the unwavering pursuit of spiritual enlightenment.

*Throughout the day, prayer becomes your steadfast companion, a lifeline connecting you to the divine realm. In the sanctuary of prayer, you pour out your heart, laying bare your hopes, fears, and aspirations before God. Through fervent supplication and heartfelt communion, you find solace, strength, and guidance to navigate the challenges that lie ahead.*

*Meditation becomes a sacred practice when interwoven with prayer, inviting you to journey inward and commune with the essence of your soul. With each moment of stillness, you dive deeper into the recesses of your being, uncovering hidden truths, and communing with the divine presence that dwells within.*

*Amidst the physical demands of fasting, you remain mindful of the needs of your body, tending to its nourishment and hydration with care and reverence. By honoring the vessel that houses your spirit, you affirm the sacred union between body, mind, and soul, fostering a harmonious balance that sustains your spiritual resilience.*

*Mindfulness becomes your guiding light, illuminating the path before you with clarity and insight. Through conscious awareness of the present moment, you cultivate a deep sense of gratitude for the blessings that grace your life, anchoring yourself in the abundance of divine grace and love.*

*As the sun sets on Day 8, you pause to reflect on the journey thus far, acknowledging the trials you have faced and the victories you have won. In the tapestry of your experiences, you discern the hand of God, guiding you ever closer to spiritual fulfillment and enlightenment.*

*In embracing the challenges of Day 8 with courage and grace, you emerge stronger and more resilient, fortified by the power of faith and the transformative grace of divine love. With each step forward, you deepen your connection with God, forging ahead on your spiritual journey with unwavering resolve and boundless grace.*

### Reflection for Journaling

- 1. Write about one positive thing that happened each day and how it made you feel.

- 2. Self-care check-in: Describe one thing you did today to take care of yourself, whether physically, emotionally, or mentally.

- 3. Future plans: Jot down one small step you can take tomorrow towards a goal you want to achieve.

- **From the insights you wrote down in your journal, write 5 prayer points to help to guide you while you pray.**

*Journal space*

### Day 9: Seeking a Deeper Connection with God.

### Scripture focus:

Psalm 42:1-2 - "As the deer pants for streams of water, so my soul pants for you, my God. My soul thirsts for God, for the living God. When can I go and meet with God?"

### Summary:

On the ninth day of our spiritual journey, we dive into the profound longing expressed in Psalm 42:1-2, where the psalmist compares their thirst for God to a deer's longing for water. This imagery vividly captures the intensity of our soul's yearning for divine connection. We are reminded of the deep, unquenchable thirst within us for the presence and sustenance that only God can provide.

As we navigate the complexities of life, we are drawn to moments of intimacy and communion with our Creator. The psalmist's cry, "When can I go and meet with God?" echoes our own desire for divine encounter. It beckons us to carve out sacred space in our lives to seek God wholeheartedly, to drink deeply from the wellspring of His presence, and to find refreshment for our weary souls.

**Analytical Enquiry and Journaling:**

- *Use your journaling space to document your insights. Afterward, use your insights to help formulate some prayer points.*

- *Reflecting on Psalm 42:1-2, consider the depth of the psalmist's longing for God's presence.*

- *Everyone at some point may have experienced what it feels like to be thirsty for the presence of God. This is often a result of being so distracted by the affairs of this world. Spend some time today and make it your number one priority to meet with God today, to quench the thirst for His presence.*

- *How does this imagery resonate with your own spiritual journey?*

- *In what ways do you thirst for God in your life?*

- *Consider moments when you have felt closest to God, like the deer finding water, and reflect on what made those experiences meaningful. Conversely, ponder times when you have felt spiritually dry or distant from God. What factors contributed to those feelings, and how can you address them moving forward?*

- *As you seek a deeper connection with God, what steps can you take to nurture your spiritual thirst and draw nearer to Him each day?*

*Journal space*

## Day 10: Prayer and Confidence

### Scripture:

Hebrews 4:16 – "Let us then approach God's throne of grace with confidence, so that we may receive mercy and find grace to help us in our time of need."

### Summary:

Day 10 centers on the powerful combination of prayer and confidence, as emphasized in Hebrews 4:16. This verse encourages us to approach God's throne of grace boldly, knowing that He welcomes us with open arms. It highlights the importance of confidence in our prayer life, reminding us that we can come before God assured of His love, mercy, and provision.

- **Confidence is a belief in oneself, abilities and judgements. It involves trust in one's own competence, worthiness and capability to handle situations effectively. Confidence often manifests as a sense of assurance, self-**

***assuredness and assertiveness in pursuing goals and facing challenges.***

*Confidence in prayer doesn't mean arrogance or entitlement; rather, it stems from a deep understanding of God's character and promises. It's an expression of faith in His goodness and faithfulness, even in the face of uncertainty or adversity. When we pray with confidence, we align our hearts with God's will and invite His intervention in our lives*

.

- ***Prayer is a cornerstone of faith, serving as the vital connection between the believers and God. It embodies both communication and communion, providing a channel to expressing gratitude, seeking guidance and surrendering to divine will.***

*Prayer is more than just a request; it's a profound conversation with our Creator, where we can pour out our hearts and share our deepest concerns. When we approach God with confidence, we acknowledge His sovereignty and trust in His ability to meet our needs. We recognize that He hears our prayers and responds with compassion and grace.*

As we reflect on Day 10, let us cultivate a spirit of confidence in our prayer life. Let us approach God with boldness and trust, knowing that He is attentive to our cries and eager to extend His mercy and grace to us in our time of need. May our prayers be marked by sincerity, humility, and unwavering faith, as we seek God's guidance, provision, and presence in every aspect of our lives.

**Reflective Question:**

- How does the idea of approaching God's throne of grace with confidence impact your prayer life and how can you cultivate greater confidence in your approach to prayer, knowing that God eagerly awaits your petitions and desires to grant you mercy and grace?

*Journal space*

## Day 11: Gratitude Journaling

### Scripture focus:

Psalm 100:4 - "Enter his gates with thanksgiving and his courts with praise; give thanks to him and praise his name."

### Summary:

While you immerse yourself in the practice of gratitude journaling, guided by the wisdom of Psalm 100:4. Let's take time to reflect on the blessings in our lives and express our gratitude to God for His goodness and provision.

Throughout the day, make a conscious effort to write down moments of gratitude in your journal. Here are ten prompts to inspire your gratitude reflections:

1. Write down three things you're thankful for today.

2. Reflect on a recent answered prayer and write about it.

3. Consider the people in your life and write about why you're grateful for them.

4. Think about a challenge you've overcome and write about the lessons you've learned from it.

5. Reflect on a favorite memory and write down what makes it special to you.

6. Consider the beauty of nature around you and write about something in nature you're grateful for.

7. Write about a small pleasure or comfort that brings you joy.

8. Consider the opportunities you've been given and write about how they've enriched your life.

9. Reflect on a moment of kindness you've experienced and write about how it touched your heart.

10. Consider the gift of each new day and write about something you're looking forward to.

**Poem:**

*In fields of grace, my heart does soar,*

*Each blessing found; I cherish more.*

*With pen in hand, I write each word,*

*Of gratitude, my heart has heard.*

*For every breath, for every ray,*

*I offer thanks, I kneel to pray. In moments still, His presence near, In gratitude, I find Him here.*

*Journal space*

## <u>Day 12: Personal Praise and Worship</u>

### Scripture focus:

Psalm 100:4 - "Enter his gates with thanksgiving and his courts with praise; give thanks to him and praise his name."

### Summary:

Today is a sacred moment, set apart for personal praise and worship—a time to bask in the glory of God's goodness and faithfulness. As we immerse ourselves in the depths of Psalm 100:4, we are beckoned to approach the throne of grace with hearts overflowing with gratitude and lips resounding with praise. This day is not just a routine of religious observance; it's a divine invitation to encounter the living God in the sanctuary of our souls, to commune with Him intimately and passionately.

### Instructions:

**1. Songs of Gratitude:** Begin this journey of personal worship by selecting songs that resonate with the melody of your heart. Let the lyrics echo the chorus of thanksgiving and adoration that reverberates within you. Through music, let your soul ascend to the heavenly realms, where praises rise like incense before the throne of God.

**2. Scripture Reflection:** Dive into the sacred pages of Scripture, where the words of life breathe hope and promise into your spirit. Meditate on passages that unveil the majesty of God's character and unveil His unwavering faithfulness throughout history. As you immerse yourself in His Word, allow its truth to penetrate deep into the recesses of your being, illuminating your path with divine wisdom and insight.

**3. Personal Testimony:** Reflect on the tapestry of your life—the threads of grace, mercy, and redemption intricately woven by the hands of a loving and compassionate God. Take a moment to recount the countless blessings and miracles that have unfolded on your journey thus far. With pen in hand or voice lifted in prayer, offer up your personal testimonies as a sweet offering of praise and thanksgiving to the One who holds your past, present, and future in His hands.

**4. Spontaneous Worship:** *Surrender to the leading of the Holy Spirit as He ignites the flames of worship within your soul. Let your praise be as natural as the rhythm of your heartbeat, flowing freely from the depths of your being. Whether in song, dance, or silent adoration, let every breath proclaim the greatness of our God and King.*

**5. Prayer of Dedication:** *Conclude this sacred time with a prayer of dedication—a surrendering of your whole being to the service and worship of the Mos High God. Offer up the desires of your heart, the dreams of your soul, and the aspirations of your spirit as a fragrant offering unto Him. May your life be a living testament of praise, declaring the glory of God to all the earth.*

*Today, as you embark on this journey of personal praise and worship, may your heart be filled to overflowing with the immeasurable love and boundless grace of our Heavenly Father. Let every note sung, every word spoken, and every moment shared be an offering of worship unto Him who is worthy of all honor, glory, and praise.*

*Journal space*

## **Day 13: Overcoming the Urge to Quit**

**Scripture focus:**

Galatians 6:9 "Let us not become weary in doing good, for at the proper time we will reap a harvest if we do not give up."

*"By now you must have felt like giving up, but you continued, nevertheless. Today, confront the common temptation to quit when faced with challenges or weariness. Drawing strength from the words of Galatians 6:9, then remind yourself of the importance of perseverance and steadfastness in the pursuit of our spiritual goals. Encourage yourself to press on, despite the obstacles that may arise, with unwavering determination, knowing that your efforts will yield a bountiful harvest in due time.*

**Instructions:**

**1. Reflective Journaling:** Take a moment to reflect on any moments during the past twelve days where you felt tempted to quit or give up. Write down these experiences in your journal, along with your *thoughts and emotions at the time. Consider what factors contributed to these feelings and how you ultimately overcame them.*


**2. Scripture Meditation:** *Meditate on the scripture from Galatians 6:9, allowing its words to penetrate your heart and mind. Consider the implications of not giving up in the face of adversity and the promise of reaping a harvest if we persevere. Let this scripture serve as a source of encouragement and motivation to keep pressing forward.*


**3. Prayer for Strength:** *Spend time in prayer, asking God for the strength and perseverance to overcome the urge to quit. Confess any feelings of weariness or doubt, and surrender them to God, trusting in His power to sustain you through every trial and tribulation. Pray for renewed resolve and determination to continue on the path set before you.*


**4. Seeking Support:** *Reach out to a trusted friend, family member, or mentor for support and encouragement. Share with them your struggles and aspirations, ask for their prayers and guidance* *as you navigate through challenges. Remember that you are not alone in your journey, and that there are others who are willing to walk alongside you.*

**5. Visualize the Harvest**: *Take a moment to visualize the harvest that awaits you if you persevere in your faithfulness and obedience. Envision the fulfillment of God's promises in your life and the abundant blessings He has in store for you. Let this vision inspire you to keep moving forward with confidence and hope.*

*As we confront the urge to quit on this thirteenth day of our journey, may we be reminded of the words of Galatians 6:9 and the promise of a bountiful harvest awaiting those who persevere. Let us press on with steadfast determination, knowing that our efforts are not in vain, and that God is faithful to reward those who diligently seek Him.*

*Bonus Text: Reflect on Jesus' experience of fasting in the wilderness, where He faced intense temptation from the devil (Matthew 4:1-11). Despite His physical weakness, Jesus remained steadfast in His commitment to the Father's will, resisting the devil's schemes with the power of God's Word. Let His example encourages you to stand firm in the face of adversity, knowing that God's strength is made perfect in our weakness (2 Corinthians 12:9).*

## Journal space

**Day 14: Sharing Your Story**

*"Today, we embrace the opportunity to share our stories of redemption and victory. As Psalm 107:2 reminds us, 'Let the redeemed of the Lord tell their story—those he redeemed from the hand of the foe.' Your journey of prayer and fasting has undoubtedly been filled with moments of divine intervention, personal breakthroughs, and encounters with God's faithfulness. Now is the time to share these testimonies with others, inspiring and encouraging them on their own spiritual journeys.*

**Instructions:**

**1. Reflective Journaling:** *Take some time to reflect on the significant moments of your journey thus far. Consider the times when God has shown up in your life, answered prayers, or revealed His presence in unexpected ways. Write down these experiences in your journal, capturing the emotions and insights associated with each moment.*

**2. Crafting Your Story:** Choose one or two key experiences from your journal entries that you feel led to share with others. Craft your story in a way that highlights God's faithfulness and the transformational power of prayer and fasting in your life. Consider how your story can resonate with and impact those who hear it.

**3. Sharing with Others:** Find opportunities to share your story with friends, family, or members of your faith community. Whether through conversation, testimony during a gathering, or written form, let your story be a beacon of hope and encouragement to those around you. Be open to God's leading as you share, allowing Him to use your testimony for His glory.

**4. Listening to Others:** In addition to sharing your own story, take time to listen to the stories of others. Pay attention to how God has been working in their lives and be a supportive presence as they share their own experiences of prayer and fasting. Remember that every story is valuable and carries the potential to inspire and uplift others.

**5. Reflective Prayer**: Close this day with a time of reflective prayer, thanking God for His faithfulness and provision throughout your journey. Pray for continued boldness and opportunities to share your story with others, knowing that your testimony has the power to bring hope and transformation to those who hear it.

As we embrace the opportunity to share our stories of redemption and victory on this fourteenth day of our journey, may we be reminded of the transformative power of prayer and fasting in our lives. Let us boldly proclaim God's faithfulness and goodness, knowing that our stories have the potential to touch hearts and change lives for His glory."

## Journal space

## Day 15: Engaged Listening

*"On this fifteenth day of our journey, we focus on the importance of engaged listening, as highlighted in Matthew 13:16: 'But blessed are your eyes because they see, and your ears because they hear.' In our fast-paced world filled with distractions, it's easy to overlook the beauty of truly listening—to God, to others, and to our own hearts. Today, we intentionally cultivate the practice of engaged listening, opening our hearts and minds to receive the messages that surround us.*

**Instructions:**

**1. Listening to God:** *Set aside dedicated time for prayer and meditation, seeking to hear God's voice amidst the noise of life. Quiet your mind and spirit, allowing God to speak to you through His Word, through the promptings of the Holy Spirit, and through moments of stillness. Listen attentively for His guidance, comfort, and encouragement.*

**2. Listening to Others:** *Practice active listening in your interactions with friends, family, and colleagues. Give them your full attention, maintain eye contact, and provide verbal and nonverbal cues that you are fully present. Seek to understand their perspectives, feelings, and needs without judgment or interruption. Show empathy and compassion as you listen, affirming their value and worth.*

**3. Listening to Yourself:** *Take time for introspection and self-reflection, tuning in to the whispers of your own heart and soul. Pay attention to your thoughts, emotions, and inner desires, acknowledging them without judgment or condemnation. Journaling can be a helpful tool for processing your internal dialogue and gaining insight into your deepest longings and aspirations.*

**4. Prayer for Discernment:** *Pray for the gift of discernment, asking God to sharpen your spiritual senses and heighten your awareness of His presence and leading. Surrender any distractions or barriers that hinder your ability to listen effectively, inviting the Holy Spirit to guide you into deeper levels of understanding and revelation.*

**5. Action Steps:** Reflect on any insights or messages you receive during your time of engaged listening. Consider how you can apply these insights to your daily life, relationships, and spiritual journey. Be open to adjusting or changes as directed by God, trusting in His wisdom and guidance.

As we commit to the practice of engaged listening on this fifteenth day, may our ears be attuned to the whispers of God's voice, our hearts open to the stories of others, and our minds receptive to the wisdom that surrounds us. Let us embrace the blessedness of truly seeing and hearing, knowing that in doing so, we draw closer to the heart of God and to one another.

*Journal space*

## Day 16: Renewed Purpose and Vision

**Scripture focus:**

Proverbs 29:18 "Where there is no vision, the people perish."

Today, we focus on renewing our purpose and vision for the journey ahead. As Proverbs 29:18 reminds us, having a clear vision is essential for navigating life's path and avoiding aimlessness. Without direction, we risk losing our way and perishing spiritually. Therefore, we dedicate this day to seeking God's guidance and clarity as we set our sights on our goals and aspirations.

**Instructions:**

**1. Reflection on Journey So Far:** Begin by reflecting on the progress made during the fasting and prayer journey. Consider the highs and lows, the insights gained, and the challenges overcome. Take note of any patterns or themes that have emerged.

**2. Clarifying Vision:** *Spend time in prayer and meditation, seeking God's guidance in clarifying your vision for the future. What are your long-term goals and aspirations? What steps can you take to align your life with God's purposes and plans?*

**3. Identifying Priorities:** *Reflect on your values and priorities, both spiritual and practical. What matters most to you? What areas of your life need greater attention or focus? Consider how you can realign your priorities to better reflect God's kingdom values.*

**4. Setting Goals:** *Based on your clarified vision and identified priorities, set specific, measurable goals for the coming days, weeks, and months. Write these goals down in your journal, along with action steps and timelines for achieving them.*

**5. Seeking Confirmation:** *Share your vision and goals with a trusted mentor, friend, or spiritual advisor. Seek their feedback and wisdom, inviting them to provide guidance and accountability as you pursue your vision.*

**6. Scripture Affirmations:** Meditate on scriptures that speak to God's promises and purposes for your life. Claim these promises as you step into renewed purpose and vision, trusting in God's faithfulness to guide and sustain you.

**7. Prayer for Direction:** Close with a time of prayer, committing your vision and goals into God's hands. Ask for His guidance, wisdom, and strength to walk in alignment with His purposes each day. Surrender any doubts or fears, trusting in His ability to lead you forward.

- Reflective Song: Take a moment to listen to your favorite worship song. Allow the lyrics to resonate with your heart as you commit your renewed purpose and vision to God.

- May this day of renewed purpose and vision propel us forward with clarity and confidence, as we seek God's direction and pursue His plans for our lives.

*Journal space*

## Day 17: The Fruit of the Spirit

**Scripture focus:**

"But the fruit of the Spirit is love, joy, peace, forbearance, kindness, goodness, faithfulness, gentleness and self-control." – Galatians 5:22-23

- Today, we explore the profound significance of each aspect of the fruit of the Spirit, as outlined in Galatians 5:22-23:

**1. Love:** Love is the foundational fruit, the essence of God's character and the driving force behind all other virtues. It is selfless, sacrificial, and unconditional, demonstrated supremely in the person of Jesus Christ.

**2. Joy:** Joy transcends mere happiness; it is a deep-seated gladness rooted in the assurance of God's presence and promises. It is not dependent on circumstances but flows from an intimate relationship with the Lord.

**3. Peace:** Peace is a tranquil state of harmony and wholeness that surpasses understanding. It is found in surrendering to God's sovereignty and resting in His unfailing love, even amidst life's storms.

**4. Forbearance (Patience):** Forbearance is the ability to endure difficulties and delays with grace and perseverance. It reflects God's patient endurance with humanity and empowers us to extend grace to others.

**5. Kindness:** Kindness is the act of showing compassion, generosity, and thoughtfulness towards others. It reflects the heart of God, who extends His kindness to all, regardless of merit.

**6. Goodness:** Goodness is moral excellence and integrity, exemplified in righteous living and honorable character. It stems from God's inherent goodness and is expressed through acts of righteousness and justice.

**7. Faithfulness:** Faithfulness is steadfast loyalty and reliability, grounded in God's unchanging nature and promises. It involves unwavering commitment to God and others, even in the face of trials and temptations.

**8. Gentleness:** Gentleness is strength under control, characterized by humility, meekness, and tenderness. It mirrors the gentleness of Jesus, who came not to conquer with force but to serve with compassion.

**9. Self-Control:** Self-control is the mastery over one's desires, impulses, and passions, exercised through the empowering presence of the Holy Spirit. It enables us to live disciplined lives, honoring God in all we do.

- Reflecting on each aspect of the fruit of the Spirit unveils the multifaceted beauty of God's character and his transformative work in our lives. Today, engage in a personal reflection and affirmation activity to reinforce the importance of cultivating these virtues:

## *Personal Reflection and Affirmation: Fruit of the Spirit Journaling*

### *Instructions:*

*__1__. Take out your journal or a piece of paper and a pen.*

*__2__. Reflect on each aspect of the fruit of the Spirit individually.*

*__3__. Write down specific ways you have seen or experienced each fruit in your life recently. Be honest and specific.*

*__4__. For each fruit, write an affirmation or declaration affirming your commitment to cultivate that virtue in your life.*

*__5__. Spend some time in prayer, thanking God for His work in your life and asking for His help to continue growing in the fruit of the Spirit.*

- *This personal reflection and affirmation exercise will help you deepen your understanding of the fruit of the Spirit and reinforce your commitment to embodying these virtues in your daily life.*

*Journal space*

## Day 18: Giving in Order to Receive (Sacrifice)

### Scripture focus:

*"Give, and it will be given to you. A good measure, pressed down, shaken together and running over, will be poured into your lap. For with the measure you use, it will be measured to you." – Luke 6:38*

*Today, we reflect on the principle of sacrificial giving and the profound truth that in giving, we also receive abundantly from God. As we explore Luke 6:38, let us deepen our understanding of the spiritual principle of sowing and reaping, generosity, and the blessings that flow from a heart willing to sacrifice for the sake of others and the kingdom of God.*

- **Biblical Principles of Generosity:** *The Bible emphasizes the importance of giving generously and sacrificially. Verses such as Luke 6:38 and 2 Corinthians 9:6-8 highlight the principle of sowing and reaping, indicating that those who give generously will also receive abundantly from God.*

- ***Stewardship and Trust:*** Christians believe that everything they have ultimately belongs to God, and they are called to be faithful stewards of His resources. By giving to others, Christians demonstrate their trust in God's provision and acknowledge Him as the ultimate source of blessings.

- ***Jesus' Example:*** Jesus Christ Himself exemplified the principle of giving to receive through His life and teachings. He taught his followers to give to the poor, care for the needy, and love their neighbors as themselves. Jesus also promised blessings to those who practice generosity, as seen in passages like Matthew 25:35-40.

- ***Joyful Giving:*** Christians are encouraged to give cheerfully and with a joyful heart, knowing that their giving is an act of worship and obedience to God. As they give to others in need, they experience the joy of knowing they are participating in God's work of blessing and transforming lives.

- **Eternal Rewards:** While Christians may receive temporal blessings as a result of their generosity, they also look forward to eternal rewards in heaven. Jesus promised that those who give selflessly will be rewarded in heaven (Matthew 6:19-21), reinforcing the idea that giving to receive extends beyond earthly benefits.

Overall, the perspective on giving to receive emphasizes the spiritual and eternal dimensions of generosity, highlighting the transformative power of giving and the abundant blessings that flow from a heart committed to serving God and others.

**Reflection Questions:**

1. How do you interpret the principle of giving and receiving as expressed in Luke 6:38?

2. Reflect on a time when you experienced the truth of this principle in your life.

3. What areas of your life are you hesitant to sacrifice for the sake of others or God's kingdom?

4. In what ways can you cultivate a spirit of sacrificial giving and generosity in your daily life?

5. How does sacrificial giving align with the example set by Jesus Christ?

6. Consider the blessings that come from sacrificial giving. How have you witnessed God's provision and abundance in your life because of your willingness to give sacrificially?

7. Are there areas in your life where you feel called to step out in faith and give sacrificially? Take time to pray and seek God's guidance in this area.

8. Reflect on ways you can encourage and support others in their journey of sacrificial giving and generosity.

- *As you meditate on these questions and the teachings of Luke 6:38, may you be inspired to cultivate a heart of sacrificial giving, knowing that as you give generously, God will pour out His blessings upon you abundantly, according to His perfect measure.*

*Journal space*

## Day 19: Prepared to Accept

### Scripture focus:

"But those who hope in the Lord will renew their strength. They will soar on wings like eagles; they will run and not grow weary; they will walk and not faint." – Isaiah 40:31

Strength is promised to those who wait and expect to receive from God. As you journey on this fast; sacrificing the flesh to strengthen the spirit man is not an easy task. One of the things highlighted in this particular verse by the prophet Isaiah, is that renewal is not partial or bias, but a resource available to those who have the courage to patiently wait on God. Strength to soar to new heights, strength to keep consistency, strength to build momentum and strength to remain focus is a promise that God will fulfill to those who hold their end of the bargain by having hope in the Lord. As you come close to the end of this journey, embrace this passage and lift your faith, it only gets better.

Today, as you reflect on the assurance of God's strength and provision, engage yourself with a reflective Word Scramble game to reinforce the key themes of this passage.

**Word Scramble Game: Reflective Unscrambling**

- **Instructions:**

1. Write down the following scrambled words related to the passage. Take your time to unscramble each word and reflect on its significance in relation to the passage. Enjoy the challenge!

   - "phoe"

   - "strgenht"

   - "wlronee"

   - "nsceutrae"

   - "itrusvopn"

     - "rnettucad"

   - "alcepeta"

   - "ptahniece"

   - "itha"

   - "ntecapice"

   - "tstreni"

- *"pce"*

- *"reath"*

- *"suimcafr"*

- *"dfenait"*

- *"tniorap"*


***Poem - Unscrambled Answers:*

In hope, we find our strength's light,

With endurance, we run our race right.

Assurance in provision's embrace,

Patience, acceptance, in every place.


Faith's unshaken stance, ever sure,

Hearts renewed, steadfast and pure.

Accepting His will, with peace's grace,

In admiration, we soar to embrace.

## Journal space

### Day 20: Ready to Receive

*"Ask and it will be given to you; seek and you will find; knock and the door will be opened to you." – Matthew 7:7.*

- *Today, as we prepare our hearts to receive from the Lord, let me share with you a story:*

*In the heart of a bustling city, nestled amidst towering skyscrapers and busy streets, there lived a widow named Hope. Despite the challenges life had thrown her way, Hope clung steadfastly to her faith in God. Her small apartment, though humble, radiated warmth and hospitality.*

*One rainy evening, as the sound of thunder echoed through the streets, Hope sat by her window, lost in prayer. Her heart heavy with burdens, she poured out her hopes and fears to the Lord, seeking His guidance and provision.*

*Suddenly, a gentle knock interrupted her prayers. Startled, Hope peered through the rain-streaked* glass to find a weary traveler standing on her doorstep, seeking shelter from the storm. Without hesitation, Hope flung open her door, inviting the stranger inside.

As they sat together by the crackling fire, Hope learned that the traveler's name was Gabriel. He spoke of his long and arduous journey, of trials faced and battles won. Hope listened intently; her heart stirred by the stranger's tale.

Moved by Hope's kindness and generosity, Gabriel revealed himself to be an angel sent by the Lord. He spoke of the countless prayers that had risen from Hope's lips, of her unwavering faith amidst trials and tribulations. "Your prayers have been heard, Hope," Gabriel proclaimed, his voice echoing with divine assurance. "Be ready, for the Lord is preparing to bless you abundantly."

With tears of joy streaming down her cheeks, Hope embraced the angel's words, clinging to them like a lifeline in the storm. In the days that followed, signs of God's favor began to manifest in Hope's life in miraculous ways. From unexpected financial *provision to divine appointments and renewed relationships, Hope witnessed the hand of God moving powerfully on her behalf.*

*And as she stood in awe of His faithfulness, Hope's heart overflowed with gratitude and praise. For she knew that in every trial and every triumph, God was with her, guiding her steps and leading her into His abundant blessings.*

*As we reflect on Hope's story, let us also prepare our hearts to receive the blessings that the Lord has in store for us. Let us trust in His timing and remain open to His guidance, knowing that He is faithful to answer our prayers according to His perfect will.*

*"Hebrews 13:2 Be not forgetful to entertain strangers: for thereby some have entertained angels unawares."*

**Question for Reflection:** How can we cultivate a heart of expectancy and readiness to receive God's blessings in our own lives?

*Journal space*

## Day 21: Embracing Renewal

*"And he who was seated on the throne said, 'Behold, I am making all things new.' Also, he said, 'Write this down, for these words are trustworthy and true.'"* – Revelation 21:5

As you come to the culmination of your journey of prayer and fasting, embrace the promise of renewal that God offers to you. Today, take the time to reflect on your transformation and commitment to continue walking in faith and obedience.

### Topic: Embracing Renewal

In this final day of your journey, reflect on the ways in which God has renewed your heart, mind, and spirit throughout these 21 days of prayer and fasting. As you look back on the challenges you've faced, the prayers you've lifted, and the moments of breakthrough and revelation you've experienced, rejoice in the work that God has done in you.

### Activities:

**1. Journaling:** Take time to journal your reflections on the past 21 days. Write about the moments of growth, the answered prayers, and the lessons learned. Express your gratitude to God for His faithfulness and provision.

**2. Prayer of Dedication:** Dedicate yourself afresh to God's purposes and plans for your life. Surrender any remaining doubts or fears and commit to walking in obedience and faithfulness in the days ahead.

**3. Celebration:** Take time to celebrate the victories and milestones achieved during this journey. Share testimonies with family, church family, friends and even co-workers encouraging one another in the faith.

**Closing Prayer:**

Heavenly Father, we thank you for the journey of prayer and fasting that we have embarked upon together. We praise you for the renewal and transformation that you have brought into our lives *during these 21 days. As we conclude this journey, we dedicate ourselves afresh to your purposes and plans. May your Spirit continue to lead and guide us, and may we walk in obedience and faithfulness all the days of our lives. In Jesus' name, amen.*

*Journal space*

*Closing Remarks:*

*As you come to the end of your 21-day journey, I want to commend you for your dedication and commitment to deepening your spiritual life. Fasting and prayer are powerful tools for transformation, and by engaging in this process, you've gained a greater understanding, clarity and connection with our Lord and Savior Jesus Christ.*

*Remember this journey doesn't end here. The insights, growth and spiritual breakthroughs you've experienced are just the beginning of an ongoing relationship with God. Continue to seek Him and allow Him to shape your path.*

*"Proverb 3:5-6 Trust in the Lord with all thine heart; and lean not unto thine own understanding. In all thy ways acknowledge him, and he shall direct thy paths."*

*Yours truly,*

Romario Smith

## Acknowledgments

*I want to express a heartfelt gratitude to everyone who has contributed to the creation of this prayer and fasting journal. I am thankful for the wisdom, guidance, and encouragement provided by Wife Shanice Dixon-Smith, colleagues and family in faith. Their insights and support have been invaluable in shaping this resource. I also extend my deepest appreciation to my readers and participants who have embarked on this journey with me. Your commitment to seeking God's presence and pursuing spiritual growth inspires me daily. inspiration. May this journal be a tool for His kingdom purposes and a blessing to all who engage with it.*

Copyright © 2024 by Romario Smith

All rights reserved. No part of this publication may be reproduced, distributed, or transmitted in any form or by any means, including photocopying, recording, or other electronic or mechanical methods, without the prior written permission of the publisher, except in the case of brief quotations embodied in critical reviews and certain other noncommercial uses permitted by copyright law.

For permissions requests or inquiries, please contact Romario Smith at romariosmith12345@gmail.com.

***Author Bio:***

*Romario Smith is an ordained minister of religion with years of experience in ministry. His dedication to spiritual leadership and guiding others on their journey of faith has been evident throughout his career. Romario's passion for empowering individuals to live purposefully and spiritually fulfilled lives has led him to write extensively on topics of prayer, fasting, and personal growth. Through his unique blend of wisdom, compassion, and practical insights, Romario has inspired countless individuals to embark on their own journeys of transformation.*